TEACHING
OTHER FAITHS

in the Catholic and Church Primary School

TEACHING OTHER FAITHS

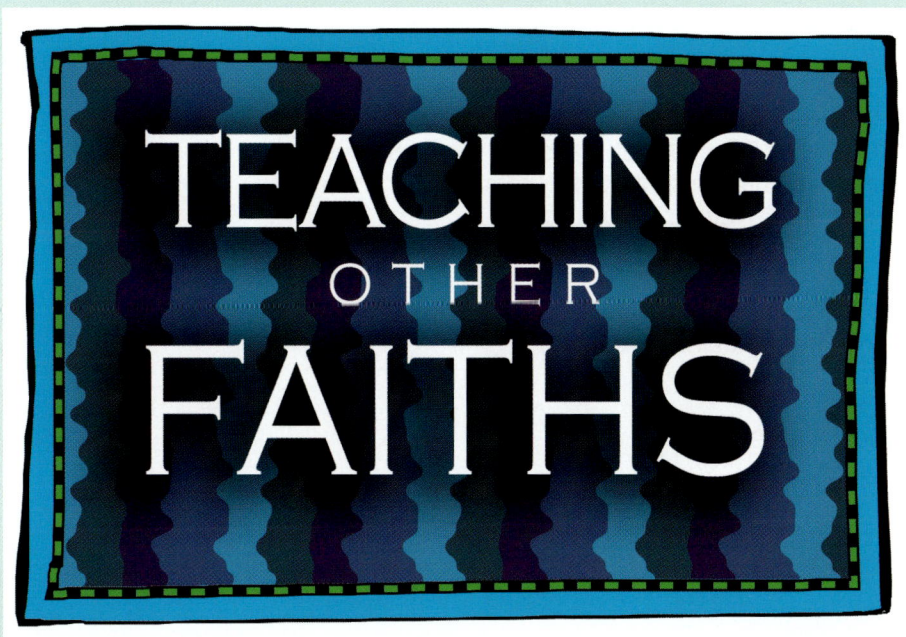

in the Catholic and Church Primary School

A teacher's guide

Victoria Hummell ra

McCrimmons
Great Wakering Essex England

First published in the United Kingdom in 2003 by
McCRIMMON PUBLISHING CO. LTD.
10-12 High Street, Great Wakering, Essex SS3 0EQ
Email: mccrimmons@dial.pipex.com
Internet: www.mccrimmons.com

ISBN 0 85597 649 7

Acknowledgements

Sr Clare Jardine NDS: friend and colleague from whom I received the first impetus to engage with the teaching of Other Faiths. Part of the section on Judaism is from a leaflet which Clare and I wrote together. Clare helped with the writing of the section on Judaism in *Here I Am*. She is currently secretary to the Bishops' Conference committee on Catholic/Jewish Relations.

Sr Simon ra: with whom I live in community, is the Diocese of Westminster east London interfaith officer. She and I have travelled up and down the country giving inservice days to teachers in various dioceses. Simon was part of the group who helped with the writing of the Other Faiths section of *Here I Am* and has kindly helped by reading this text.

Sr Mavis Langmead RJM: friend and colleague. Mavis and I spent time together at Hengrave Hall working on the very first conception of the idea of a section on Other Faiths in *Here I Am*. She was part of the writing working party.

Fr Ieuan Wyn Jones, former director of Religious Education of the Archdiocese of Cardiff who was also part of the writing working party for the Other Faiths section of *Here I Am*.

All the teachers I have met on inservice days who are so enthusiastic and hard-working and who desire to equip their pupils for life in a global multifaith society.

Cover design and page layout by Nick Snode
Main text set in 12pt Tahoma, main headings set in 60pt Flyer Black Condensed
Text pages printed on 100gsm matt art, cover printed on 260gsm one sided art
Printed and bound in England by Thanet Press Ltd., Margate, Kent

Contents

Introduction

This guide has been written as a result of requests from primary teachers who have attended inservice days given in various dioceses in England and Wales.

The revised version of the Bishops' Conference National Project programme *Here I Am* [1] contains a detailed programme of study of other faiths. This is the first time that a Catholic primary programme has included such a study.

The guidance offered here is based on that programme of study.

Teachers have sometimes expressed some concerns such as their own lack of knowledge, fear of confusion for pupils, protocol for visits to places of worship and parental reaction. It is hoped that this guide will address those concerns as well as being a handy and quick reference for teachers. It does not supply all that one needs to know about a faith, there are many excellent books and web sites that do that.

The term *other faiths* is used throughout this guide, because the reference is to faiths other than the Catholic faith. Other faith teaching is not to be confused with multicultural education, which is threaded through the entire curriculum and also may be present in the teaching of other faiths.

In many schools Catholic pupils will belong to a number of different cultural groupings, which are respected and celebrated in the life of school.

The *Religious Education Curriculum Directory for Catholic Schools* [2] makes it clear how the study of other faiths is an important part of religious education. It details the following areas of study at key stage 2:

- ◼ "respect for the writings and holy people of other faith communities in England and Wales." [3]

- ◼ "respect for celebrations of other faith communities and appreciation that prayer has a place in their life." [4]

- ◼ "ways in which care for others is important for other faith communities... that other faith communities have codes of behaviour based on their beliefs." [5]

---

1   Published by Collins, 2000.

2   Published by the Bishops' Conference of England and Wales through Catholic Education Service, 1996.

3   The Church: page 21.

4   Prayer: page 29.

5   Love of Neighbour: page 37.

The Catholic Church and other faiths   1

Before the Second Vatican Council (1963-65), the Church's concern with other faiths was limited to its thinking about the problem of salvation for those "outside" itself. Vatican II revealed a major shift in the Church's attitude. Catholics are called to be committed to respecting people of other faiths and to recognise that God is at work in them. The opening words of the document *Gaudium et Spes* expresses well our common humanity:

> *"The joy and hope, the grief and anguish of the people of our time… are the joy and hope, the grief and anguish of the followers of Christ as well."* [6]

Another important document from Vatican II was *Nostra Aetate* (Declaration on the Relation of the Church to Non-Christian Religions):

> *"In this age of ours, when people are drawing more closely together and the bonds of friendship between different peoples are being strengthened, the Church examines with greater care the relation which she has to non-Christian religions. Ever aware of her duty to foster unity and charity among individuals, and even among nations, she reflects at the outset on what people have in common and what tends to promote fellowship among them.*
>
> *"All people form but one community. This is so because all stem from the one*

> *stock which God created to people the entire earth (cf Acts 17: 26) and also because all share a common destiny, namely God…*
> *"The Catholic Church rejects nothing of what is true and holy in these religions. She has a high regard for the manner of life and conduct, the precepts and doctrines, which, although differing in many ways from her own teaching, nevertheless often reflect a ray of that truth which enlightens all. Yet she proclaims and is in duty bound to proclaim without fail, Christ who is the way, the truth and the life…' (John 14:6). In him, in whom God reconciled all things to himself (cf 2 Corinthians 5:18-19), people find the fullness of their religious life. The Church, therefore, urges her children to enter with prudence and charity into discussion and collaboration with members of other religions. Let Christians, while witnessing to their own faith and way of life acknowledge, preserve and encourage the spiritual and moral truths found among non-Christians, also their social life and culture."* [7]

Our shared goals have been marked by events like the gathering of faith leaders with the Pope at Assisi in 1986 and again in Rome in 1999. After the prayer for peace at Assisi, Pope John Paul said:

---

6   *Gaudium et Spes* 1 in Vatican Council, page 903, Flannery, Costello, 1975.

---

7   *Nostra Aetate* 1-2 Vatican Council, page 738-739, Flannery, Costello, 1975.

"Every authentic prayer is called forth by the Holy Spirit, who is mysteriously present in the heart of every person." [8]

This knowledge marks profoundly the Church's attitude towards those of other faiths. The Church teaches that, while living out our Christian faith, we are called to listen to, and dialogue with, those of other faiths. Above all, we must respect their integrity and dignity, recognising that "*seeds of the Word*" [9] can be found outside the visible structures of the Church. We may find we can learn from those of other faiths.

In more recent Church documents, Christians are directed to both witness and dialogue. This means entering into relationships with people of other faiths. Asking people of other faiths to come and talk about their religion to our children is a very good way of making friends and paving the way for future good relationships. This is what the Church calls the "dialogue of life"; co-operation, respect for one another's convictions and traditions, and learning from one another in a very human way. [10] The Church teaches that, whilst living out our Christian faith, we are called to listen in dialogue and be ready to learn from those of other faiths, many of whom may, in our multi-cultural society, be our neighbours.

The Bishops of England and Wales in *Catholic Schools and Other Faiths* (1997) [11] suggest that schools need to:

"find ways in which pupils can learn to engage in dialogue and to develop an attitude of respect for religious diversity. This will necessitate the inclusion of a broader study of both Christianity and of other world faiths in the Religious Education syllabus"

and again in the same document:

"The aim of Christian education – at whatever level – remains what it has always been: to be formed in Christ with a mature and strong sense of the Christian missionary vocation. Nowadays, however, the Church sees this as including the capacity for entering positively into relationships with neighbours who belong to other religious traditions.

"At the very least this will entail learning about such communities – their beliefs, traditions, religious practices, etc. But it may also mean learning from them, through encounter and dialogue at various levels. In a multi-faith society it is becoming increasingly important for Christians of all ages to reflect positively on the inter-faith relationship and to learn the correct and discerning use of the two principles discussed above. A faithful witness to Christ does not preclude but positively demands that Christians learn to respect and to listen to what the other wishes to say to us. Though the emphasis may vary, depending on circumstances, the tension between faithfulness and openness must always be maintained. To attempt to teach one without the other would be both theologically and pedagogically inadequate." [12]

8   Pope John Paul II address at the World Day for Peace, Assisi 27th October 1986.

9   *Redemptor Hominis*, John Paul II, 4th March 1979 n.11.

10   Cf *Redemptoris Missio*, 1990 nn 55, 57.

11   Page 22, the Bishops' Conference of England and Wales, published by Matthew James 1997.

12   Ibid page 14.

Basic principles and approaches   2

The teaching of other faiths at the level of primary-aged children is about how the members of that faith community live as a family and how they worship. It begins from the faith community's own understanding of itself and what it is to be a member of a particular community.

How?

Each faith is taught separately from other faiths. Sometimes in the past other faiths have been taught through a theme such as *light*, looking at what light might mean in different faiths. This method leads to confusion and comparison. It does not do justice to the integrity of each faith. The other faith is now taught without comparison to any other faith, although that is not to say comparisons will not arise, but that will not be the starting point of the teaching. Ideally pupils will have an opportunity to meet with people of other faiths and to visit their place of worship. However where this is not possible, the internet, videos and books may provide support. (See section 7 on Visitors and Visiting, and section 8, Resources).

The recommended approach in *Here I Am* is to teach other faiths for five hours or two weeks per year, one in each of the two longest terms of the school year so there is no diminishment of delivery of the religious education programme. In *Here I Am* each lesson begins with *Look*, this is an opportunity for pupils to consider their own experience; for instance a special building in the locality, the hospital, library etc. This is followed by *Learn*, the main part of the lesson where pupils may for instance learn about the function of the mosque. In the plenary pupils are encouraged to *respect and appreciate* how important the mosque is for Muslims.

When to start?

Some schools may begin to teach about other faiths in year one, some may want to start in the reception class. At key stage 1 it might be expected that pupils will consider some aspect of faith life which is significant for the people of that faith, eg how a faith community prays as a family.

At key stage 2 it might be expected that pupils will consider how faith plays an important part in the lives of individuals, families and communities. Pupils will be encouraged to understand the importance of showing sensitivity, respect and appreciation for feelings of people who hold religious beliefs different from their own. They may gradually begin to be familiar with the stories celebrated at certain festivals and acquire a knowledge and appropriate vocabulary for worship, beliefs and festivals.

Which faiths?

It is important always to teach Judaism:

"since Christians and Jews have such a common spiritual heritage." [13]

The second faith may be chosen from Hinduism, Islam or Sikhism, depending on which is the most common faith community in the locality. Where there is no other faith present, the school may wish to choose Islam, as it is a world faith that many people follow.

Collective Worship

During the week on other faiths, it would be good if there were prayers offered for the people of that faith. During the week on Judaism it would be very appropriate to use psalms or stories from the Hebrew Scriptures (Old Testament) which we share with our Jewish brothers and sisters. It is not appropriate to use worship which rightly belongs to another faith, for example, to perform puja[14] or to use the action that Muslims use in their worship.

Stories from other faiths may also be inappropriate as they may lead to confusion in the mind of pupils. Catholics cannot worship as anything else but Catholics. If the gathering is not an act of worship but is quite clearly a *show and tell* assembly then it would be good for pupils to tell each other what they have learnt about another faith.

Assessment

Attainment target 1, which is *learning about*, represents no difficulty; it is content led, which is the main component of the Other Faiths programme of study. Attainment target 2 *learning from* is more problematic; at the end of each lesson pupils are encouraged to respect and understand but may not necessarily *learn from* the other faith in the way they would from their own faith, which has an application to their daily life.
Care needs to be taken to teach the other faiths in a detached way.
The use of the pronoun *they* rather than we is important.

Parents and Governors

Teaching other faiths in the Catholic primary school is relatively new.
If it has not been in the experience of some governors or parents they may be rather concerned.
Like anything new it is important that enough information is given, in the religious education newsletter and the religious education co-ordinator's report to governors.

---

13   *Nostra Aetate* 4 Vatican Council, page 741, Flannery, Costello, 1975.

14   See section 4 on Hinduism.

Invite parents and governors into school during the other faiths week so that they can see the work of the pupils. Try to involve parents in visits to places of worship. Sometimes parents' fears are about the unknown, or in an area of social deprivation where there are problems about housing it may be more about that.

Stereotyping

It is true that people of certain faith groups may also belong to the same cultural grouping, but it is not always possible to place people into faith communities based on appearance and dress. Some groups may interpret the rules of their belief in different ways, some may include cultural customs which are not strictly part of their religion. The BBC video *Pathways of Belief* show a variety of Jewish and Muslim children looking different but all speaking with lovely Scottish accents.

3 Judaism

Why teach Judaism?

More than with any other faith, Christianity has a special relationship with Judaism and shares the same roots. Despite their closeness and shared heritage the relationship has been burdened by a long history of persecution and misunderstanding. We now want to develop a positive attitude for the future where there is an appreciation and a deeper knowledge of Jews and Judaism.

What is Judaism?

Judaism is the oldest of the three monotheistic faiths. The way it is observed today has developed over the centuries. The Old Testament tells how the Hebrew people began to believe in the One God who called them into a special relationship. In time their religious practices became centred on living according to God's *Torah* (teaching) and worship in the Temple in Jerusalem.

Jesus of Nazareth was a Jew who lived during the time of the Second Temple (the first having been destroyed when the people went into exile in 724 BCE[15]). At the time of Jesus there were many groups within Judaism. Each group held certain beliefs and practices according to their interpretation of the oral traditions. Discussions and debate among the groups were very common and according to the Gospels Jesus seems to have been involved in them.

Mezuzah
A mezuzah is a small container that holds a scroll on which the shema is written. It is placed on the door post of Jewish homes. (see: Deut.. 6:4-9)

Rabbinic Judaism, the forerunner of modern Judaism, began after the Romans destroyed the Second Temple in Jerusalem in 70 CE[16] (AD), a few decades after the death of Jesus. The sacrificial system came to an end and the rabbis adapted the Temple worship to the synagogue (literally, a meeting place) and the home. Many Jewish festivals and special days (eg *Shabbat*) are kept in the home as well as in the synagogue.

---

15 BCE (Before the Common Era).

16 CE (Common Era).

Shofar
Ram's horn.

The rabbis kept Judaism alive and wrote down the oral traditions with all their interpretations. Until this day Jews engage in debate about how laws and teachings should be interpreted in new situations.

Different kinds of Jews

Different branches of Judaism have emerged as a result of different ways of interpreting the Bible and the traditions. Orthodox Jews hold a stricter view and don't believe that laws can be adapted to meet the demands of modern life. On the other hand, Progressive Jews (Liberal and Reform) think that some laws and teachings can be interpreted more freely. Judaism is not just a religion but is also a mark of cultural and ethnic belonging, so some Jews regard themselves as secular rather than religious Jews.

What do we have in common with the Jewish people?

Christianity owes much of its rich heritage to Judaism. The first Christians were Jews who, like Jesus, observed the Jewish traditions. Certain beliefs, prayers and traditions were held onto and became part of Christianity when the two groups eventually parted.

Menhora

The menhora is a seven-branched candlestick which symbolises the candelabrum which was lit daily in the Temple when it was still standing.

It is now the emblem of the state of Israel.

Beliefs

One of the key beliefs both Jews and Christians hold is the One God who is the creator of all and who holds all things in his love. Some scriptural verses which express this faith, the *Sh'ma*[17], are recited during the weekly *Shabbat* service in the synagogue. Christians too believe in One God but hold that God is manifested in three persons. From the shared belief in One God comes a sharing in the gifts of creation and the responsibilities that come with that. Another key belief

17   This can be found in Deuteronomy 6: 4-9.

for both Christians and Jews is in God's revelation at Sinai when the people of Israel received the law. The Ten Commandments to which Christians adhere are part of that law, thus Christians and Jews have shared values and morals.

Prayers

Many of the blessings and prayer formulae, which are so familiar to Christians, have their origins in Judaism. The Lord's Prayer (or Our Father) contains many phrases and words, which come from Jewish prayers. The blessings with which Christians sanctify bread and wine are almost identical to the sanctification blessings pronounced by the Jewish people before the *Shabbat* meal on Friday nights in their homes.

The Torah scrolls are written in Hebrew and contain the first five books of the Bible.

Traditions

Although the yearly cycle of festivals contains many differences, there are some elements which Jews and Christians share.
One important similarity is that both traditions have a period of time set aside each year for individuals to reflect on his/her relationship with God and fellow human beings and to put right any wrongs done. Repentance and a belief in God's love and mercy are key features of both Judaism and Christianity.

Scripture

Jews call the Scriptures *Torah* or *T-N-K*, an acronym which stands for the three sections in the Hebrew Bible – the Torah, the Prophets and the Writings. The arrangement of the books differs from the Christian Old Testament and there are slightly fewer books than in the Catholic Bible. Christians have tended to interpret the Old Testament in the light of their faith in Jesus Christ. Since Jews do not hold this faith, their interpretation of the Hebrew Bible is very different.
For them it is complete in itself and interpreted in the writings of the rabbis throughout the history of the Jewish people. The Church calls on Catholics to respect and appreciate this belief.

Judaism should be taught as a religion in its own right. It needs special attention because of the intrinsic relationships between it and Christianity. Our very roots lie in Judaism. Jesus was a Jew as were his first followers. However, while it is important to teach about the Judaism at the time of Jesus, this should be taught separately from modern Judaism as another faith.

What about worship?

We cannot pray as Jewish people but we can pray for the well-being of Jews. We can thank God for the variety and richness that Judaism brings to our world. The Hebrew scriptures (Old Testament) are familiar to both Jews and Christians alike. When we use the psalms we are sharing with our Jewish brothers and sisters.

Can we have a Passover meal in school?

This special rite can only be celebrated by Jewish people. If Christians re-enact this it is not a celebration of the rite but an experience to deepen understanding and respect. It is best to invite a rabbi or observant Jew to re-enact it for you (see the appendix).

The Shabbat Meal

What follows is a simple format for a Shabbat meal. Sometimes the men would have gone to synagogue first and then returned home for the start of Shabbat.

Shabbat starts on Friday evening at home when there are three stars in the sky or when you can hold your hand before your face and not see it, although these indicators would be difficult to register in the modern city. The Shabbat is welcomed as a queen. People greet each other. Everything is prepared beforehand. The house is cleaned, the meal is ready. The meal starts with the following ritual:

1 **Lighting the candles**
Mother lights the candles, moving her hands round the flame several times then in front of her face, to welcome in the Sabbath:

Baruch atah adonai elohenu melech ha-olam asher kidshanu b'mitzvotav v'tzivanu l'hadleek ner shel shabbat.

Blessed are you, Adonai our God, ruler of the world, who makes us holy through doing his commandments and commands us to kindle the Sabbath lights.

Continued ▶

The Shabbat Meal continued

2   **Blessing the children**
The father or grandfather lays their hands on each child's head and says:

Girls: *May God make you like Sarah, Rebecca, and Leah.*

Boys: *May God make you like Ephraim and Menasseh.*

For all children: *May God bless and keep you.*

*May God's face shine on you
and be gracious to you.*

*May God's face be lifted upon you
and give you peace.*

3   **Kiddush blessing over the wine** (*the cup is held in the right hand*):

Baruch atah adonai elohenu melech ha-olam borei p'ree hagfen.

*Blessed are you, Lord our God, ruler of the world,
    who creates the fruit of the vine.
Blessed are you, Adonai, ruler of the world,
    who makes us holy with mitzvoth and shows us favour.
You have made us holy by giving us your commandments
    and have shown us your favour.
With love you have given us your Sabbath
    which recalls the work of Creation.
This day is the first of the holy festivals recalling our going forth from Egypt.
You have chosen us from all the people and made us holy
    and you have shown us your loving favour
    by giving us Your holy Sabbath as a heritage.*

Baruch atah adonai m'kadesh ha-shabbat.

Blessed are You Lord our God, who sanctifies the Sabbath.

The wine is drunk.

4   **Handwashing**
At this point everyone washes their hands; this is intended to show the spirituality of this time and the importance of good preparation.

5   **Blessing of the bread**
(*the two challah loaves are held up*):

Baruch atah adonai elohenu melech ha-olam ha-motzi lehem min ha-aretz.

*Blessed are you, Lord our God, ruler of the world,
who brings forth bread from the earth.*

The bread is eaten sprinkled with salt.

Havdalah (separation)

The end of the Shabbat on Saturday night is signalled in the same way as the start. The following ceremony is observed:

1 **Kiddush**

   The wine cup is filled to overflowing allowing, some wine to spill on the dish. The desire is for the blessings of Shabbat to overflow into the coming week. The cup is raised:

   Baruch atah adonai elohenu melech ha-olam borei p'ree hagfen.

   Blessed are you, Lord our God, ruler of the world,
   who creates the fruit of the vine.

2 **Blessing of the spices**
   The spice holder is lifted:

   Baruch atah adonai elohenu melech ha-olam borei minay v'samim.

   Blessed are you Lord our God, ruler of the world,
   who creates all kinds of spices.

   Each person sniffs the spices and remembers how good the Shabbat was.

3 **Blessing over the Havdalah candle**

   Baruch atah adonai elohenu melech ha-olam borei m'oray ha-esh.

   Blessed are you, Lord our God, ruler of the world,
   who creates the lights.

   The candle is lit and held in the right hand.

The final prayer is about Havdalah separation.
The twilight hour has passed and the new week has begun.

   Blessed are you, Lord our God, ruler of the world, who makes a distinction
   between the sacred and secular, light and darkness, Israel and other people,
   the seventh day and the six days of labour.

   Everyone takes a sip of wine, the candle is put out in the wine on the plate.

4 Everyone wishes each other *Shavua tov*, a happy week.

4 Hinduism

Origins

Hinduism is one the world's oldest religions. It has its origins in the Indus Valley civilization.

The word Hindu is a western word which grew from the Persian name for the people who lived beyond the river Indus, pronounced *Hindu*.

About 85 per cent of the population of India is Hindu. It is estimated that about five hundred thousand Hindus live in Britain.

The religion

Hindu god Ganesha.

Hinduism is a family of religions rooted in the Indian sub-continent, which means that there is great variety in what is counted as Hindu practice and beliefs. It is a monotheistic religion with one god who is Brahman. Brahman is the origin of all creation, part of the inner and outer world, pure delight, intelligence and pure being.

Brahman has three major qualities or trimurti (three gods), Brahman, Vishnu the preserver, and Shiva the destroyer.

Hanuman.

Vishnu came to earth in human form, an *avata*, to destroy evil. Two famous avatars are Krishna and Rama.

Shiva is the lord of the dance, both destroyer and preserver. Krishna is often depicted as a cow herd playing the flute. Rama is the hero who fought evil. Hanuman is the monkey god. Ganesha the elephant god is the son of Shiva and Sita. He is very popular as he stands for

Aum

Aum is a sacred symbol which is chanted as a mantra.
It is said to represent the first sound of creation.
Its chanting brings calmness and a feeling of being in touch with the gods.

the removal of obstacles, for strength, protection and good fortune. The murti (gods) are often depicted with blue faces, a sign of holiness.

Most Hindus accept the idea of karma, that is good actions which will lead to a cycle of birth and death, samsara. Heaven is reached and the cycle of birth, life and death is ended when Brahman and the soul are united. This concept of reincarnation is not one that is taught to primary-aged pupils.
The Vedas are a collection of hymns and writings gathered together from around 1500 BCE.[18] The concept of a loving deity led to the writing of the Bhagavad Gita, The Song of the Loving Lord.

Worship

The Hindu place of worship is called a mandir or temple. Hindus do not have any particular day for worship, but in England will gather at the weekend and for special festivals. Much worship takes place in the home.

At home each family has its own shrine. Normally the mother of the family is responsible for it. It may be in a spare room or a corner of the kitchen. Each day, or three times a day for the devout, the family will perform puja.

In front of the shrine there is a puja tray with a bell, tumbler of water, spoon, deva lamp, incense and holder, container of kum kum powder, flowers, food.
What follows is a very simplified version of puja; it will vary with the customs of the family:

Stage 1

The bell is rung and a chant *Aum* is sung. Everyone joins in to remove any bad tendencies and invoke good ones, to make a protective shell around the worshippers.

Stage 2

To bring god to mind by chanting sacred texts. *Mantras of invocation.*

Continued ▶

---

18 BCE (Before Common Era).

Worship continued
(Simplified version of Puja)

Stage 3

This is a time of making offering to the god whose being is installed in the image present so that the spiritual force of the god flows towards the people.

1 Water is sprinkled over the image.

2 Offering of sandal paste mixed with kum kum; with this a dot is put on the forehead of the god and the worshippers.
Flowers are offered.

3 Incense and lights are offered to the gods by waving them in a circular motion from the right side: fruit and food is offered. The light is taken to each person as reminder of the eternal light of spirit shedding its glory on everyone. This is called arti.

Stage 4

The sending back of the god invoked for the ritual and the protective shell is broken. Finally the entire puja or worship is dedicated to the Supreme Lord Brahman.

Family

Each child is brought up to perform meditation, worship family gods, show respect for elders, give hospitality and show respect for living creatures. Hindus are normally vegetarian.

Caste

There is no teaching about caste, which is less important than in previous times, or about the belief in reincarnation at the primary stage.

Islam 5

Origins and belief

Islam is a monotheistic religion. The Arabic word islam literally means 'surrender' or 'submission' and comes from a word meaning 'peace'. In a religious context it means complete submission to the will of Allah. Muslims call God 'Allah'. They believe that everything and everyone depends on Allah. In theory, all that is necessary for one to become a Muslim is to recite sincerely the short statement of faith known as the *shahadah*: *"I witness that there is no god but Allah and that Muhammad is the Messenger of God."*

Muhammad (pbuh)[19]

In an historical sense Muslims regard their religion as dating from the time of Muhammad, in a religious sense they see it as identical with the true monotheism which prophets before Muhammad, such as Abraham (Ibrahim), Moses (Musa), and Jesus (Isa), had taught. In the Qur'an, Abraham is referred to as a Muslim. The followers of these and other prophets are held to have corrupted their teachings, but Allah sent Muhammad to call people yet again to the truth. Allah's last prophet was Muhammad (pbuh). He was a man through whom God revealed his will. He was born in 570 CE at Mecca in Arabia. At that time in Arabia idolatry was common. Muhammad worked first as a trader, and gained a reputation for honesty. Muhammad (pbuh) often spent time alone reflecting. In 610 he had his first revelation, a vision of the angel Gabriel (Jibril), who told him that he was to be a prophet. Over many years Muhammad received the text of the Qur'an in a series of revelations. With small groups of people who

19 Muhammad is so esteemed by Muslims that it is usual to utter the blessing, "Peace be upon him" after his name. This is often abbreviated to "pbuh".

believed what he said Muhammad began to spread the message. Muhammad publicly condemned the existing idolatrous local beliefs, and religious customs, He formed a tribe of those who accepted him as the Prophet, and gradually Islam grew in strength and acceptance.

The Qur'an

Muslims are guided to follow Allah's will by the Qur'an, which they regard as the unaltered word of God. It is written in Arabic. They treat this book with reverence, never touching it without washing their hands and they never put it on the ground, or put other books on top of it.

The five pillars of Islam

Every Muslim must perform the duties known as the Five Pillars of Islam:

1. **Faith**
   – that is to believe in Allah and Muhammad (pbuh) his prophet.

2. **Salah**
   – to pray five times a day.

3. **The 'Zakat'**
   – to give alms to the poor.

4. **The Fast**
   – to fast at Ramadan.

5. **Pilgrimage** (Hajj)
   – if possible to make the pilgrimage to Makkah.

Salah – Worship

The Muslim place of worship is called a mosque. The word comes from the Arabic for "place of prostration". Muslims attend the mosque on Friday, their holy day.
All mosques have a minaret from which the call to prayer is given.
A translation of that call is as follows:

God is most great.
God is most great.

God is most great.
God is most great.

I testify that there is no god except God.
I testify that there is no god except God.

I testify that Muhammad is the messenger of God.
I testify that Muhammad is the messenger of God.

Come to prayer!
Come to prayer!

Come to success (in this life and the Hereafter)!
Come to success!

God is most great.
God is most great.

There is no god except God.

On entering the mosque everyone covers their head. There is a place where people can deposit their shoes and go to wash before going into the prayer hall. Inside the prayer hall there are no seats, but the floor is covered in carpet. The only decoration is that of calligraphy or geometric designs. Men and women worship in separate parts of the mosque. People pray facing Makkah.

Continued ▷

Crescent moon and star

A common cultural symbol in the Islamic world is the crescent moon and star. Often used in decoration and can be seen on the top of minarets of the mosque.
The moon represents the fact that the Muslim calendar is based on the movements of the moon.

When people refused to believe in Allah, Muhammed would point to the sky and ask them who they thought made the stars.

Prayer at home

Muslims pray five times a day and follow a special ritual to do so. Children pray at home with their parents who teach them how to pray.

Preparation for prayer:

Firstly they wash (wudu).
The water must be pure: if there is no clean water sand may be used. This involves a special process…

❖ Wash hands up to the wrist three times.

❖ Wash mouth three times.

❖ Wash nostrils, breathing in and out through the nose three times.

❖ Wash arms up to elbows three times.

❖ Wipe head with wet hands, forehead to back, back to forehead. Rub outside the ears with wet fingers, inside with wet thumbs at the same time.

❖ Wash feet up to the ankles three times.

❖ Raise one's face to the sky, pointing up with the index finger.

Shoes are removed before prayer and the head is covered.
Prayers can be said anywhere as long as it is clean and preferably quiet. They will face in the direction of Makkah, a very holy place for Muslims. A prayer mat may be used. There are certain prayer positions which remind Muslims of how they should be before Allah:

1. *Standing*
   – being upright and well behaved.

2. *Bowing*
   – showing respect for Allah.

3. *Prostrating*
   – being ready to do Allah's will.

4. *Kneeling*
   – being thankful.

The prayers are said at the same time each day:

- **Fajr** – Morning, between dawn and sunrise.
- **Zuhr** – Mid-day or early afternoon.
- **Asr** – Late afternoon.
- **Maghrib** – Evening, around sunset.
- **Isah** – Night, before going to bed.

Some festivals

Ramadan

For one month each year Muslims fast as part of a special time for prayer and self-examination.

'Eid Al Fitr'

This religious festival marks the breaking of the fast and the end of the Muslim holy month of Ramadan.

6 Sikhism

Origins

Sikhism is the newest world religion. It was started in the Punjab by Guru Nanak in 1499 who founded it within the background of Hinduism and Islam. Today the largest Sikh community outside India is in Britain.

Beliefs

Sikhs believe in one God, *Nam* (name), who cannot take human form. They believe in the teachings of the ten Gurus and the scripture, The Guru Granth Sahib. A Guru is a teacher or leader. Life is a continual cycle of life and rebirth: reincarnation.

The Mool Mantra sums up the basic belief of the Sikhs. Guru Granth Sahib begins with the Mool Mantra. Every Sikh is expected to recite it daily. The English translation is given below beside each original:

Ik Onkaar.	*There is only one God.*
Sat Naam.	*His Name is Truth.*
Karta Purkh.	*He is the Creator.*
Nir Bhau.	*He is without fear.*
Nir Vair.	*He is without hate.*
Akaal Moora.	*He is beyond time (Immortal).*
Ajooni.	*He is beyond birth and death.*
Saibhang.	*He is self-existent.*
Gur Parsaad.	*He is realised by the Guru's grace.*

The Mool Mantra.

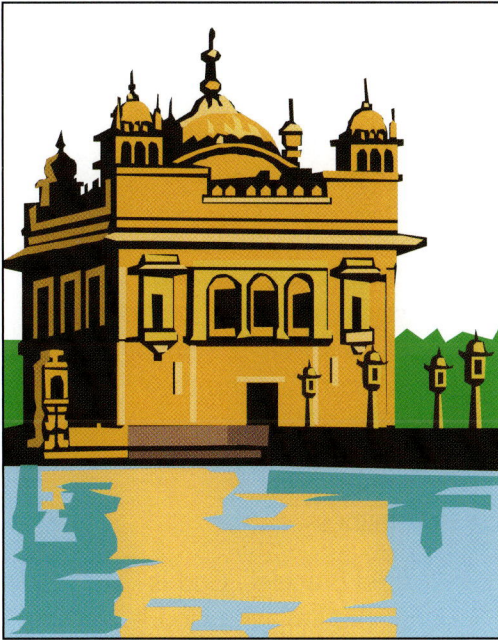

*Gudwara
(Temple)*

*– Golden
Temple of
Amritsar.*

Sikhism preaches universal equality: men and women are equal.
It regards all religions and people as equal before the eyes of God.
Sikhs are expected to live humbly at the service of others, be truthful, promote family life, to earn their living in service of some kind and to share with the poor.

Khanda symbol

This is an important symbol of the beliefs of Sikhs.

Circle, showing God has no beginning or end.

Two swords remind Sikhs they fight for justice and truth and they symbolise God's spiritual and worldly power.

Khanda, belief in one true God, a two-edged sword for freedom and justice.

Guru Nanak

❖ Guru Nanak was born in 1469 in Punjab, and brought up as a Hindu. When he was 30 years old he disappeared for three days and was taken to Heaven in a vision and given *amrit* (nectar) to drink. God asked him to be a guru. He spent the next 20 years travelling around preaching. He collected disciples/Sikhs around him. Nine gurus followed Guru Nanak.

❖ 2nd **Guru Angad** developed the Sikh language *Gurmukhi*.

❖ 3rd **Guru Amar Das** opened the *langar*/kitchen.

❖ 4th **Guru Ram Das** founded the holy city of Amritsar.

❖ 5th **Guru Arjan** built the golden temple at Amritsar and collated the first scriptures *Adi Granth*. He was the first Sikh martyr.

❖ 10th **Guru Gobind Singh**, the last human guru, who established the *Khalsa*.

❖ 11th and last Guru, is the scripture *Adi Granth,* also known as the ***Guru Granth Sahib***.

The Khalsa

The festival of Baisakhi celebrates the founding of the Khalsa by Guru Gobind Singh. Its origin is explained by the story of the Five Faithful who volunteered to die for their faith. Those who belong to the Khalsa follow a strict code of discipline: they serve God in any way necessary, recite five hymns each day, avoid alcohol, must not steal, commit adultery or gamble.

They must especially serve all poor. The members of the Khalsa, who may be men or women, wear the five special signs:

1. *Kesh* — unshorn beard and hair covered by a turban, a sign of holiness and dedication to God.

2. *Kirpan* — a sword, the willingness to overcome spiritual and physical oppression. Often Sikhs will wear a symbol of a sword around their neck.

3. *Kangha* — a comb, to show cleanliness.

4. *Kara* — a steel bracelet, God is one, the link with God is unbreakable.

5. *Kachera* — shorts, to show readiness to defend Sikhism.

Worship

The most significant historical religious centre for the Sikhs is the Golden Temple at Amritsar in the state of Punjab in northern India. However all places where Guru Granth Sahib are installed are considered equally holy for Sikhs. The Sikhs call their place of worship a gurdwara. They do not have a particular day for worship. People remove their shoes and cover their head. As people enter the gurdwara they bow before the Guru Granth Sahib and leave an offering. Men and women sit on the floor on separate sides. Care needs to be taken that feet are kept tucked under as it is an insult to point feet at the Guru Granth Sahib which is

Reading the Guru Granth Sahib.

kept on a cushion under a canopy. During worship the Guru Granth Sahib is read by either a man or a woman who waves a Chauri over it, a whisk made of horsehair, as a mark of respect The service consists of the reading, singing and meditating on the Guru Granth Sahib. Parshad, sweet holy food stirred by a kirpan (sword) is taken at the end of the service, as a reminder of the sweetness of God.

An important aspect of worship is the hospitality in the Langar, a free community kitchen that can be found at every Gurdwara. There meals are served to all people of all faiths. Guru Nanak first started this institution which outlines the basic Sikh principles of service, humility and equality.

Some festivals

Baisakhi: founding of the Khalsa.

Divali: festival of lights symbolising inner light and remembrance of Guru Hargobind(6th) being released from prison.

Gurpurbs: birthday of Gurus Nanak, Gobind Singh and martyrdom of Guru Arjan. Guru Granth Sahib is read aloud to the congregation over a period of 48 hours.

7 Visitors and visits

Visitors

If there is a member of another faith community on the staff or among the parents it would be very good to use them. If you invite a member of a faith community into school from outside it is important to ensure that they are well briefed as to the age, ability and previous knowledge of the pupils and given exact details of what you would like them to do. It is a good idea to ask them to demonstrate something rather than give a lecture. Eg, ask a Jewish visitor to demonstrate a Shabbat meal, a Muslim to show the postures adopted for prayer, a Hindu to demonstrate a puja ceremony or a Sikh to show pupils the signs of the Khalsa. The pupils need to be well prepared to welcome, show respect and have questions prepared for the visitor.

Visits

A visit to a place of worship is a very effective way of teaching about another faith. Make sure you have visited first yourself and made it clear to your host the age and needs of your pupils. It would be useful to ask your host what the exact requirements are in terms of dress code that should be observed for girls and boys. In order to benefit from the visit, pupils need to be well prepared to know what to look for and to understand the respect required in such a place of worship. In the synagogue boys will be expected to cover their heads. In the mosque, gurdwara or mandir everyone will be required to remove their shoes and cover their heads. When going to a mandir it will be necessary to check that the time you have chosen is a time when the gods are on display. There are certain times of day when they rest from public view. In the gurdwara you will be offered hospitality in the langar. This will be vegetarian. It would be good to make sure you give the gurdwara an offering.

Whether you have had a visitor or gone on a visit to a place of worship, do not forget to check whether there is any fee involved. It is always good practice to get the pupils to write a 'thank you' card.

Resources 8

Ritual objects

The term *ritual objects* is used rather than artefacts as it says more of their function and of the respect with which we treat them. Some of these need to be bought to enhance the understanding of another faith. Care needs to be taken in their handling and use because we wish to respect the importance and reverence with which people of other faiths treat their holy objects. It is possible to obtain *soft sets*[20] for younger children of: a synagogue, Shabbat meal, a Sikh man etc. These may be handled and played with as they are different from actual objects such as for instance, a Muslim prayer mat.

The following is a list of suggested resources necessary for teaching each of the other faiths. The web sites need to be checked as they may have changed and are only given as an example. It is useful to check sites about other faiths using a search engine.

Judaism

Year 1	- A simple Bible story book.
Year 2a	- Visit by a Jewish person or a video about Shabbat.
	- 2 candlesticks and candles.
	- Kiddush cup – a special cup of wine.
	- Challah bread.
	- Cover for the bread – either home-made or bought.
	- Havdalah candle (candle with several wicks).
	- Spice box – home-made or bought.
Year 2b	- Visit to synagogue or a video (Jewish Education Bureau).
	- Kippah (small skull cap).
	- Small reproduction Torah scroll or picture (Christian Education Movement).

Year 3   - Simple Bible,

- Mezuzah case (small box fixed to door(s) of house).

Year 4   - Simple Bible,

- visit to synagogue or video about synagogue or scroll,

- Tailit (prayer shawl),

- a couple of examples of cards for Bar/Bat Mizvah.

Year 5   - Visit by Jew or watch a video of Pesach (Passover),

- 2 candlesticks and candles and kiddush cup if re-enacting,

- Seder plate Special food.

Year 6   - Apples and honey,

- a couple of examples of Rosh Hashanah (Jewish New Year) cards,

- simple Bible,

- picture of Shofar (ram's horn) (CEM[21]).

General

- Books about Shabbat, Synagogue, Pesach, the Sefer Torah (Scroll), The High Holy Days (Rosh Hashanah and Yom Kippur),

- some background books for teachers (CEM),

- pictures (CEM),

- Access to internet, examples:

  www.theresite.org.uk
  www.jewmusm.ort.org
  www.vtorah.com

Hinduism

Year 1   - Picture of or ritual objects used in the Hindu home shrines,

- Hindu doll or pictures of Indian dress,

- rakhi or bracelet.

Year 2a   - Picture of Hindu home shrine,

- Puja set or picture of one, (a puja set contains the following: metal tray, incense stick, bell, tumbler of water, small spoon, diva lamp with five wicks, kum kum (red) powder),

- a model or picture of one of the gods,

- grains of rice,

- flowers (see folder),

- picture of Rama.

Year 2b   - Divali card,

- video or picture of Divali,

- picture of a rangoli pattern or template,

- rakhi or bracelet.

---

21   Christian Education Movement; the address is included at the end of this section.

Year 3	- Books, - video and/or pictures of Krishna, Vishnu and Shiva.
Year 4	- Visit, - books, - video and/or pictures of a mandir (temple) and Ganesh, - ingredients to make *prasad* (recipe on p483 of HIA).
Year 5	- Books with Hindu stories, - sample of Sanskrit writing.
Year 6	- Picture or ritual object of the symbol *Aum*, - tape/CD of Hindu mantras, - information about Ghandi, - story of Rama, - picture, book or video of *Benares* on the Ganges.
General	- Books about Hinduism, - stories of special Hindu people, - some background books for teachers (CEM), - pictures (CEM), - access to internet, examples: www.theresite.org.uk www.hindu.org www.hindunet.org.uk

Islam

Year 1	- picture of Muslims praying, - prayer mat.
Year 2a	- Visit to a mosque or a video or picture of one, - a copy of the Qu'ran or picture, - a Qu'ran stand and cover, - picture of Muslims praying.
Year 2b	- Picture of Muslims praying, - prayer mat, - subhah (prayer beads), - 99 beautiful names of Allah.
Year 3	- Books, - video about Muhammad, - a copy of the Qu'ran or picture of a page of Arabic writing, - visit from an Imam or video.
Year 4	- List of prayer time for Muslims, - Id-ul-Fitr card.
Year 5	- Atlas, - picture, video clip of Mecca.
Year 6	- Some food marked *halal*.

General - Books about Muhammad,

- Mecca,

- mosque,

- Ramadan,

- the Qu'ran,

- Muslim prayer,

- Some background books for teachers (CEM),

- Pictures (CEM),

- Access to internet, examples:

  www.theresite.org.uk
  www.ummahp.org.uk/
  sitemap.html
  www.cie.org

Sikhism

Year 1 - Visit a Gurdwara, or show a picture or a video of a Gurdwara.

Year 2a - Visit to, picture of or video of a Gurdwara,

- picture of a Granthi reading the scriptures,

- a chauri (special fan) or picture of one.

- picture of a gutka (prayer book).

Year 2b - Picture of Guru Nanak, or a picture of 'ik Onkar' (see folder).

Year 3 - Picture, books and/or video of Guru Nanak.

Year 4 - Stories of the Gurus, especially Har Rai (7th Guru).

Year 5 - Ritual objects,

- video, picture of the five Ks:
  1   kesh, turban (uncut hair)
  2   kirpan, sword
  3   kangha, comb
  4   kara, steel bangle
  5   kacha, shorts

- picture of Sikh flag.

Year 6 - Visit, picture, video and/or books about the Gurdwara and the Golden Temple at Amritsar,

- some Divali cards.

General - Books about the Gurus,

- Sikh people,

- the Gurdwara,

- Some background books for teachers (CEM),

- pictures (CEM),

- Access to internet, examples:

  www.theresite.org.uk

  www.sikhs.org

Other useful resources:

❖ Faith communities themselves.

❖ **Study Centre for Christian –
   Jewish Relations**
   34 Chepstow Villas
   London, W11 2QZ
   Tel: 020 7229 6266

❖ Education Officer
   Council of Christians and Jews
   5th Floor
   89 Albert Embankment
   London, SE1 7TP
   Tel: 020 7820 0090

❖ **The National Society's
   RE Centre**
   36 Causton Street
   London, SW1P 4AU
   (Same address for the SHAP
   calendar of Religious Festivals).

❖ **Christian Education
   Movement** (CEM)
   Royal Buildings
   Victoria Street
   Derby, DE1 1GW

❖ *Religions in the UK
   – a Multifaith Directory*
   published by the Inter Faith
   Network is in some libraries and
   gives addresses.

❖ **The Inter Faith Network
   for the United Kingdom**
   5–7 Tavistock Place
   London WC1H 9SS
   (It also publishes a short list of local
   Interfaith councils).

❖ **LEA Resource Centres**

❖ **Public libraries**

❖ Some dioceses have Interfaith
   Offices/Centres

❖ ITV/BBC Schools Programmes

❖ Internet

9 Bibliography

Title	Publisher	ISBN No
For teachers		
Documents of Vatican II	Costello 1975	
Catholic Schools and Other Faiths	CES 1997	
Religions of the World	Collins	0-00-471008-8
World Religions	Lion Access Guides	780745-950631
Children – general		
All Kinds of Beliefs	Sadie Fields Productions Ltd	1-85707-505-6
Judaism		
The Seventh Day is Shabbat	Heinemann	0-435-30401-1
A Day to Rest	RMEP	1-85175-182-3
My Jewish Faith	Rainbows	0-237-51897-X
JUDAISM – A Pictorial Guide	Christian Education Movement	1-85100-093-3
Jewish	Watts	0-7496-2059-5
Jewish Synagogue	Keystones	0-7136-4338-2
Special Occasions	Wayland	9-780750-222730

Title	Publisher	ISBN No

Hinduism

Title	Publisher	ISBN No
My Hindu Faith	Evans Brothers Ltd	0-237-51896-1
A Row of Lights	RMEP	1-85175-183-1
Hindu Mandir	Keystones	0-7136-5495-3

Islam

Title	Publisher	ISBN No
My Muslim Faith	Evans Brothers Ltd	0-237-51898-8
Muslim Mosque	Keystones	0-7136-5344-2
Something to Share	Heinemann	0-435-30401-1
Exploring Islam	Christian Education Movement	1-85100-014-3
Watching for the Moon	RMEP	9-781851-75207-2
Islam – A Pictorial Guide	Christian Education Movement	1-85100-071-2
Teaching RE – 5-11: Islam	Christian Education Movement	1-85100-106-9
Muslim	Watts Books	0-7496-2058-7

Sikhism

Title	Publisher	ISBN No
My Sikh Faith	Rainbows	0-237-51980-1
A Birthday to Celebrate	RMEP	1-85175-185-8
Sikh Gurdwara	Keystones	0-7136-4834-1

10 Appendix

A Christian–Jewish Relations Publication reproduced with permission.

Christians and the Passover Seder Meal

In recent years many Christian groups have organised a demonstration Seder meal, primarily to understand better the Last Supper of Jesus and the roots of the Christian Eucharist. As Cardinal Hume said, "[We] have become more profoundly conscious of the Jewish soil that nourished our Christian roots. We cannot hope to understand Jesus Christ and the significance of his life and teaching without knowledge of his people, their history and beliefs." The Passover is an ancient Jewish festival which is still celebrated enthusiastically by Jewish people. The purpose of this leaflet is to provide background information and guidelines to ensure that the distinctive Jewish character of the Seder is fully respected by Christians.

What is a Passover Seder?

The Hebrew term *Seder* means "order" and refers to the whole celebration, which can last for several hours, during which the Jewish people commemorate and re-live, as a family or a community, their liberation from Egypt: *"We were slaves to Pharaoh in Egypt and our Eternal God led us out from there with a mighty hand and an outstretched arm. If the Holy One, ever to be blessed, had not led our ancestors out of Egypt, we and our children and our children's children would have remained slaves to Pharaoh in Egypt"* (The Passover Haggadah).

The most important part of the Seder is the story of God's liberation of the Israelites from Egypt and this account is commonly called *Haggadah*, a term that means "*the telling*". This is based on the biblical commandment, "*Thou shalt tell thy son in that day saying 'It is because of that which the Lord did for me when I came forth out of Egypt'* " (Exodus, 13: 8). The story is not simply a reading from the Bible but is interspersed with episodes from later Jewish tradition and contemporary struggles for freedom are included. According to the scholars the *Haggadah* as it is known today as a separate liturgical text was first drawn up around the ninth century of the common era, but the rites and prayers are much older, going back to the pre-Christian era.

Ritual food

Various ritual foods which symbolise the Exodus are eaten – *matzah* (unleavened bread), green and bitter herbs and haroset (a sweet mixture).

The role of children

Children play an important part and the ceremony is designed to hold their interest. The youngest child asks the questions that introduce the narrative. A game is played and lively songs round off the evening.

Jesus and the Passover Seder

The New Testament records that Jesus observed the Passover every year (cf Luke, 2: 41 ff) and all the Gospels connect the Last Supper with the Passover festival. In New Testament times, the rite consisted of the offering of the lamb in the Temple of Jerusalem and the family (or group) eating it as a feast in "memory" of God's liberation of the people from oppression in Egypt. However, the Evangelists say nothing about the manner of celebrating the Passover. Their main purpose was to explain the new significance they believed Jesus had given to the rite and the early Eucharistic practice of the Church is reflected in the Gospel text. In any

case the Last Supper was different from the Passover Seder as it is celebrated today. From the historical point of view, we cannot definitely affirm from the New Testament that Jesus' Last Supper was a Passover meal. Some scholars would tend to see it rather as a farewell meal.

However, the authors of the New Testament agree in interpreting Jesus' death on the cross and his testament-memorial transmitted during the Last Supper: "Do this in memory of me" (Luke, 22: 19) in the context of Passover.

The Eucharist and the Passover Seder

The New Testament situates the origin of the Christian Eucharist, which is the memorial of the death and resurrection of Jesus, in the context of Passover. However, the Eucharistic practice of the Church is also intimately linked with the Jewish prayer of blessing said on many occasions in daily life, especially before and after meals. Mark (14: 22-23) clearly refers to the blessings over bread and wine: "He took bread and blessed and broke it ...then Jesus took a cup and when he had given thanks, he gave it to them". The same Hebrew term *b'rach* means both to bless and give thanks.

The grace after meals is said to be of biblical origin. It consists of four blessings which thank God for food, for the land, for redemption from Egypt and for the covenant and revelation of the Torah. It is preceded by a summons to pray and a dialogue between the host and participants. At special meals, like the Passover and the Sabbath, a cup of wine is drunk after the Grace.

Can Christians celebrate the Seder?

Since it is a constitutive rite of Judaism, the Passover can only be celebrated by Jews. But Christians can benefit by understanding and appreciating this celebration. The ideal way is to be invited to a Passover Seder as a guest of Jewish friends in their home. Thus one would be truly a "guest" of the Jewish tradition and faith to which the Church is "linked in its very identity" (Pope John Paul II).

When Christians re-enact the Passover Seder it is not a celebration of the rite but a reflection and a learning experience to deepen understanding, in respect and gratitude. When this is done it is advisable to invite a rabbi or an observant Jew who is conversant with the tradition. A preparatory meeting to explain the rite can be very helpful.

Bishops' Guidelines on the Passover meal

The Bishops' Conference of England and Wales give this directive in the Guidelines for pastoral activity during Holy Week:

"In recent years the custom has grown in many parishes to arrange a demonstration Seder during Holy Week. This can have educational and spiritual value. It is wrong, however, to
'baptize' the Seder by interspersing it or concluding it with New Testament readings or Christian associations - or, worse, turn it into a Eucharist or a prologue to a Eucharist. Such mergings show a lack of respect for Judaism and a distortion of both Christian and Jewish traditions.

"The primary reason why Christians may decide to hold a demonstration Seder should be to understand better the Jewish roots of our Eucharistic liturgy. Any sense of 'restaging' the Last Supper is inappropriate, historically inaccurate and should be avoided.

"Demonstration Seders arranged in co-operation with local synagogues are strongly encouraged. Wherever possible, a Jew should be invited to lead the Seder and assist the Christians present to understand its ritual and meaning to the Jewish community …In all events, Christians should take every care to ensure that the correct Jewish ritual is followed and that the Seder be respected in its full integrity."

This text is published by the Study Centre for Christian-Jewish Relations.

For further information contact:
The Study Centre for Christian-Jewish Relations,
34 Chepstow Villas,
London W11 2QZ
Tel/Fax 020-7229 6266